Blessed are they
who keep his statutes and seek him
with all their heart.

PSALM 119:2

THE FIRST STEP BIBLE SEEK & FIND LEARNING BOOK
published by Gold'n'Honey Books
a part of the Questar publishing family
© 1994 by Questar Publishers, Inc.
Illustrations © 1994 by Joe Stites
Designed by David Uttley

International Standard Book Number: 0-88070-668-6

Printed in the United States of America

For information:
QUESTAR PUBLISHERS, INC.
POST OFFICE BOX 1720
SISTERS, OREGON 97759

96 97 98 99 00 01 02 — 10 9 8 7 6 5 4 3 2

THE FIRST STEP BIBLE
Seek & Find
LEARNING BOOK

By L. J. Sattgast
Illustrations by Joe Stites

Gold 'n' Honey BOOKS

See What God Made

God made the world and the plants and animals. And God made us. Thank you, God!

*Guess who I am!**

raccoon   stork   bear   elephant

CAN YOU FIND

1

PRICKLY PORCUPINE?

tiger   watermelon   giraffe   ladybug

The Water is Gone

God kept us safe
in the big, big boat.
But now we are glad to be out!
*Guess who we are!**

*NOAH, HIS FAMILY, AND ALL THE ANIMALS, GENESIS 6–9

rhinoceros   parrot   puddle   monkey

WHAT CAN YOU FIND THAT IS

Green

dove   lizard   turtle   rainbow

Our Own Little Baby

God promised to give us a little baby boy.
And here he is—Oh, how we love him!
*Guess who we are!**

*ABRAHAM & SARAH, GENESIS 18, 21

moon   firefly   blanket   branch

CAN YOU FIND

2

WOOLLY SHEEP?

owl   rabbit   tent   bat

God Tells Me What to Do

God told me to save some grain.
And now everyone has
enough to eat!
*Guess who I am!**

*JOSEPH, GENESIS 41

sack of grain   bee   pyramid   table

CAN YOU FIND

3

PLAYFUL KITTENS?

bread   scoop   basket   scarf

Baby in a Basket

I watch my brother floating in the basket.
Will he be safe? Yes! God will
send the princess to take care of him.
Guess who we are!

crown   duck   baby Moses   necklace

princess   dragonfly   Miriam   frog

Crossing the Water

We do not know how to get across the water.
So God makes a path for us.
And we never get wet!
*Guess who we are!**

chicken   grandpa   cooking pots   cow

CAN YOU FIND

4

HAPPY CHILDREN?

flower   wagon   grandma   crab

Someone Calls My Name

One night I think I hear Eli calling me.
But Eli says to listen carefully.
He says that God is the One calling me!
*Guess who I am!**

pillow

Samuel

dog

candle

HOW MANY CAN YOU FIND?

Eli

pitcher

bed

cup

Stronger Than a Giant

Goliath is big.
Goliath is strong.
But God makes me stronger!
*Guess who I am!**

sling

soldier

Goliath

spear

CAN YOU COUNT

5

SMOOTH STONES?

sword   David   King   helmet

God Takes Care of Me

Look what is coming!
God knows that I am hungry.
So He sends some birds with food
to take care of me.
Guess who I am!*

grapes   berry bush   apple   salamander

CAN YOU COUNT

6

BLACK BIRDS?

Elijah   carrot   grasshopper   banana

Where Lions Are

The lions are hungry.
But they will not bother me.
God's angel keeps me safe.
*Guess who I am!**

angel   ladybug   cloud   lion

WHAT CAN YOU FIND THAT IS

Orange

chain   wall   sun   Daniel

The Best Gift Ever

God's angel told me that
I would have a baby. And now
here He is! Little baby Jesus.
*Guess who I am!**

*MARY WITH JOSEPH, LUKE 1–2

Baby Jesus   bird   sheep   stable

WHAT CAN YOU FIND THAT IS

Blue

Joseph   Mary   straw   horse

Something Good to Hear

What is this bright light?
It is angels telling us about a baby.
The baby is God's Son,
and we want to see Him!
*Guess who we are!**

*SHEPHERDS, LUKE 2

harp   shepherd   pouch   sheep

CAN YOU FIND

7

BRIGHT ANGELS?

camp fire   staff   log   sheep dog

Follow the Star

From far away we followed a star, until we found what we were looking for—Baby Jesus! *Guess who we are!**

*WISE MEN, MATTHEW 2

camel   ring   treasure chest   star

WHAT CAN YOU FIND THAT IS

Purple

wise man   Bethlehem   grass   gift

Looking for Someone Special

I told everyone that someone special was coming. And now, here He is—JESUS! *Guess who I am!**

*JOHN THE BAPTIST, MARK 1

rope

river

Jesus

sandals

CAN YOU COUNT

8

CAT TAILS?

rock   doll   John the Baptist   palm tree

Going Fishing

I try and try but I cannot catch any fish.
Jesus tells me where to fish,
and see how many fish I catch!
Guess who I am!*

*SIMON PETER, LUKE 5

pelican   Peter   fish   bucket

WHAT CAN YOU FIND THAT IS

Brown

net   snail   dock   boat

My Little Lunch

I'm glad I gave my lunch to Jesus.
Now everyone has enough to eat!
*Guess who I am!**

*A LITTLE BOY, JOHN 6

lunch bag   water pot   bread   grass

CAN YOU FIND

9

BASKETS OF FOOD?

boy   ant   cat   flowers

Come Close, Little Ones

We want to see Jesus.
Does Jesus want to see us?
Oh yes! Jesus loves us very much!
*Guess who we are!**

wheel

bouquet

door

cantaloupes

HOW MANY

CAN YOU FIND?

girl   house   oranges   bow

Up Here I Can See!

Even though I am small, I can see Jesus from this tree. And Jesus can see me! *Guess who I am!**

squirrel

leaf

nest

Zacchaeus

Yellow

plant   window   caterpillar   laundry

Hosanna to the King!

Why are we happy?
Why do we shout, "Hosanna"?
Because Jesus is coming this way.
*Guess who we are!**

cap   corn   gate   barrel

CAN YOU COUNT **10** PALM BRANCHES?

donkey   spider   coat   sack

Happy to See Jesus

When Jesus was hurt, I was sad.
But now Jesus is alive.
Oh, happy day!
*Guess who I am!**

*MARY MAGDALENE, JOHN 20

road   cross   stone   sunrise

WHAT CAN YOU FIND THAT IS

Red

butterfly   empty tomb   fox   tulips